HOME DEFENDER

Contents

FORWARD
BY

MT. STERLING CHIEF OF POLICE
DAVID CHARLES

TO PROTECT AND SERVE

It continuously amazes me that in today's society we attempt to make preparations for advancing at work, we schedule our children's time in sports and events to the point that they are no longer allowed to simply play, even the family dinner and conversation has fallen prey to our hectic schedules.

In this mad rush we have happily assigned our safety to others to be concerned with, as we no longer have "time" for such trivial matters.

We expect our government to be prepared for any eventuality that may arise and promptly mediate this without injury to anyone including the criminals who precipitated the event.

Whenever a tragedy unfolds the initial reaction is almost always, "how was this allowed to occur and why didn't the authorities stop it before it did."

This ignores the facts that many family members, friends, and neighbors were just too preoccupied to notice the warning signs.

Home Defender; By Steve & Eva Challis

I cannot encourage you strongly enough to take the time to develop safety plans for yourself and your family. The time you take to prepare today may save your lives in the future. Wouldn't you rather look back and think, "Thank God we took time to prepare" as opposed to "If only I had…" This includes many facets of safety, internet security, drug use, fire plans, disaster planning, power outages; and yes, physical danger due to criminal violence.

It is a sad fact that some people choose to prey upon other members of our communities for their personal gain. You must develop a plan for this just as you would if there was a fire. In my opinion a firearm is an integral part of this plan.

I'm sure almost everyone is familiar with the old adage; don't take a knife to a gunfight. This is just another way of saying you should be prepared.

I firmly believe in every American's right to own firearms as individuals and encourage this.

I was fortunate in that I was raised in a family and community where firearms were not only present but often used for sport and recreation and spoken of. I was taught their safe use and handling along with the possibility that if needed I may have to utilize one in the defense of my family.

Home Defender; By Steve & Eva Challis

Sadly many times in my career as a law enforcement officer I have observed the aftermath when these basic tenets are not followed. In many circumstances tragedy could be avoided if only the victim had taken the smallest precautions by being armed in order to defend themselves.

I was excited when Steve asked me to review his latest work, Home Defender. I have enjoyed his previous works and looked forward to this one as well. I must say he has not disappointed me with it either. It is a must read for anyone new to the idea of protecting themselves and family. He covers all of the most commonly asked questions that I have encountered.

In addition to the beginner it will also serve as a much needed refresher to the more experienced as well, as too often we become complacent.

Enjoy the following pages and as you read them, quiz yourself on how prepared you are in an honest manner. After you have finished, develop a plan. By doing so you can give Steve the greatest gift he desires by allowing him to help ensure you and yours are safe and secure. Steve still lives by our creed, "to protect and serve" and does so daily in his commitment to educate.

In closing I'd like to welcome you to the world of firearms.

I have made many great friends over the years based upon a common interest and it is always a pleasure to have more people join.

Mt. Sterling, KY
Chief of Police
David Charles

Home Defender

By Stephen Challis &

Eva Challis

"The right to defend one's home and one's person when attacked has been guaranteed through the ages by common law."

- Martin Luther King

Introduction

It has been a good night; the kids have finally fallen asleep after bickering and arguing for over an hour. It is almost midnight and Debbie is more than ready for bed.

Being a single parent was never easy but all in all she is coping well. She had purchased a handgun for protection and a digital gun safe for it that she kept in the bedroom, to prevent her children getting access to it. A quick check around the house, check the door locks, and the alarm system.

All was OK.

She crawls into bed, and read a couple of pages of her book. Finally Debbie is warm and settled.

Switching off the bedside lamp she settles down to sleep. Listening to the ticking clock getting fainter and fainter as her brain reviews the past day's events and looks forward to tomorrow's agenda. Suddenly she is awake again and her eyes wide open.

She heard a strange unfamiliar sound that she cannot immediately place. She listens more intently. Her first thought is that maybe one of the kids is up and around, but this sound is outside the house.

She sits up and tries to pin point the sound. Then she hears a footstep and the unmistakable rattle of the back door. It dawns on her that someone is outside.

Then there is a moment of quiet. Debbie relaxes, it's probably a drunk, or someone lost. Thankfully she remembered to lock the door. Then there is the unmistakable sound of the rear door glass being broken. She panics and sits upright then grabs for the phone. It is dead, no dial tone.

Instinctively she turns on the light and tries the phone again, still dead. Her Cell phone should work, but it was in the kitchen on the charging unit.

Hurried footsteps outside the door make her drop the phone. The door bursts open and a tall dark figure enters the room. He is holding a gun and it is pointing straight at her.

The man speaks; *"Don't scream honey, do exactly what I say and you will not be hurt."*

This scene is played out for real at numerous times across our nation.

The risk of home invasion has prompted many homeowners to consider strategies of self-defense.

These may take the form of installing a new alarm system, fitting new locks, and perhaps buying a large dog.

All of these will obviously help discourage break-ins, but it is a sad fact that there are still high levels of crime in the US. Statistics change but the following from 2005 give a guideline.

One property crime happens every 3 seconds

One burglary occurs every 10 seconds

One violent crime occurs every 20 seconds

One aggravated assault occurs every 35 seconds.

One robbery occurs every 60 seconds or 1 minute

One forcible rape occurs every 2 minutes

According to a United States Department of Justice report, 38% of assaults and 60% of rapes occur during home invasions. One out of every 5 homes will experience a break in or home invasion, that's over 2 million homes.

In chapter 2 we will revisit Debbie and analyze the mistakes and omissions that led to her perilous situation.

Home Invasion

The term "Home invasion" has been used broadly to describe any crime committed by an individual unlawfully entering a residence while someone is home. More narrowly, home invasion has been used to describe a situation where an offender forcibly enters an occupied residence with the specific intent of robbing or violently harming those inside.

So what does the law say? The definition in law can vary, and the limited numbers of states incorporating the term "Home Invasion" into their state statutes include the intent on the part of the offender in their definition.

In part, these statutes have defined intent as--

*A person enters or remains unlawfully in a dwelling with the intent of committing a violent crime.

*A person knowingly enters the dwelling place of another with the knowledge or expectation that someone (one or more persons) is present.

*The unauthorized entering of any inhabited dwelling or other structure belonging to another with the intent to use force or violence upon the person of another.

Public perception and media reports of home invasion do not necessarily include intent for this reason.
TV anchors often question why a case was dismissed or a light sentence was given to an offender. The police are

constrained by law. Unless the facts fit certain definitions, then the law says a crime has not taken place.

Of course this is all very well if you are a lawyer or Police officer. If not; you only know that someone has forced their way into your home with intent to do you or your family harm. This leaves the homeowner with certain decisions to make.

In his book "More Guns Less Crime" John Knott makes a compelling case for the use of a firearm in defending yourself, your family, and your home. Packed with facts and statistics it has been acclaimed by academics and law enforcement.
However, there are still many politicians and gun control advocates that reject his claims. Whenever a

mass shooting occurs their voices are
the loudest. And if you have had a
son or daughter shot while at school,
it is only natural to blame the gun. A
natural but flawed reaction.

The guns used to kill so many
children and others at recent mass
shootings were all operated by human
beings; as are the guns used by the
Police and our armed forces, every
day to keep us safe.

At the NRA convention in Houston in
2013, broadcaster Glenn Beck held up
a Brown Bess musket used initially by
the Redcoats in the war of
Independence.
Captured by Colonial forces this same
gun was then used against them
before being lost in battle along with
its new owner.

~ 19 ~

Picked up off the battlefield the gun
again changed hands and was used
again by insurgents against US troops.
Later acquired by a collector, this gun
is now held by the NRA Museum
from where Mr. Beck borrowed it.
The musket has a fascinating history,
but that was not why Mr. Beck held it
up to the crowd. He did so while
asking a simple question.
"Is this a bad gun or a good gun?

I have not yet met a gun control
advocate who can answer the
question. Of course the answer is
clear enough to all but the extreme
gun ban advocates; it is neither.
It is a gun; as good or bad as the
person using it. No more or no less.
The AK 47 semi-automatic rifle has
the dubious reputation of being

responsible for more deaths than any other weapon. This so called fact is often repeated, even on pro-gun shows and documentaries which is pure fiction. Strangely enough, despite extensive research, I cannot find one case of an AK47 loading and pointing itself at a person then shooting them by pulling its own trigger.

All guns require a human to operate them, either in person or remotely. Take away the human and the AK47 becomes an inert piece of metal. This may seem obvious to most people but somehow certain lawmakers seem quite unable to grasp it.

So having dispelled the idea that guns are solely responsible for mass killings, let us turn to their use as a defensive weapon.

Training Qualifications; Steve Challis

Certified Instructor, National Rifle
Association, (NRA) Life Member

Home Firearm Safety
Personal Protection in the Home
Shotgun
Rifle
Pistol

Certified Instructor, Kentucky
Concealed Carry Deadly Weapon,
(CCDW)

Training Qualifications; Eva Challis

Certified Instructor, National Rifle Association, (NRA) Life Member

Home Firearm Safety
Personal Protection in the Home
Shotgun
Rifle
Pistol

Certified Instructor, Kentucky Concealed Carry Deadly Weapon, (CCDW)

CHAPTER ONE

OWNING A FIREARM

Bill of Rights
Amendment II

"A well regulated militia, being necessary for the security of a free State, the right of the people to keep and bear Arms, shall not be infringed."

So reads the Second Amendment of the Constitution of the United States. This grants the citizens of the USA the legal right to own and use firearms.

It does not differentiate between good or bad citizens, nor does it restrict the right to only an armed militia, despite what the anti-gun lobby insist. There are well over 1 hundred million gun owners in the USA, and many of these owners own more than one gun. This statistic alone is scary enough, but adds to it the fact that the Police do not have a legal duty to defend you, and then it is no wonder the public fear gun violence.

However, most gun owners are not criminals and they own guns for a wide variety of reasons. Certainly not all are members of the NRA, which at the time of writing has just over 5 million members.

Since moving to the United States from Great Britain, (where the use of firearms for self-defense has been outlawed since 1926) I have been aware of a fact that I had not really considered before. Having a firearm on your person not only keeps you safer, it also makes you feel safer.

This is a very important distinction. I find myself going out in the dead of night, on our isolated farm, to investigate suspicious noises with fewer reservations. Something I would never have considered in England. I feel well trained and competent to use my firearm, and perhaps more importantly, when not to.

In 2008 I moved to Alaska and married my wife Eva. At that time Eva worked for the US Forest Service in Ketchikan Alaska. I was 59 years old and some 2 weeks shy of my 60th birthday.

Eva lived in a small modular home at the foot of a tall snow covered peak called Deer Mountain. A year before, at the time we got engaged, I had attempted to climb it but the severe winter conditions prevented me from doing so.

Now it was late fall and the conditions were better. I decided that if I was ever going to climb the mountain, it was now or never.

I set out at 7 am carrying just light supplies.

Among these were Eva's 357 revolver and a few spare rounds. Eva had insisted I take it, as there are both black bears and wolves on the mountain. This information would have been enough to have kept me firmly away, but somehow the knowledge that I had the gun on my hip dispersed any concerns.

I was about two hours into my climb and feeling pretty good, and I still had about two thousand feet to go when I was stopped in my tracks. Something was ahead of me. I heard a low growl; it was coming from the clump of bushes ahead of me. I knew I was a long way from the town and any help. I unclipped the revolver strap and took firm hold of the gun. I still had no idea what the creature was, but it sounded larger than a dog.

Eva had told me that bears will normally run from humans, I knew that, but was unsure if anyone had informed the bears.

After a few moments I heard the sound of something moving away.

After about 3 or 4 minutes I relaxed and moved on. I never saw the bear but I can honestly say I never considered aborting the hike. I finished it without incident.

Later I moved to Kentucky and Eva and I became active in the fight for gun rights. We established a shooting school and I became a life member of the NRA and a certified firearms instructor both with the NRA and the State of Kentucky.

Eva followed suit and I found myself getting deeper involved with the gun rights lobby, appearing at gun rights rallies and on TV as well as radio.

After obtaining our Concealed carry permits we regularly carried guns with us as we travelled around the USA.

In 2011 we were travelling back from an NRA convention. We had been on the road for several hours and pulled into a road side rest area to use the rest rooms and change drivers. I was not really thinking of guns or personal defense as I stepped out of a cubicle in the rest room to be confronted by 4 black men. All of them were in a huddle discussing something. When they saw me, they stood up and lined up in front of me blocking my exit.

I slowly slid my right hand into my pocket and gripped my Walther PPK pistol. The movement was immediately noticed by the 4 men who followed it with their eyes. I did not draw the weapon but stood facing them. After exchanging glances, the men moved aside and allowed me to exit.

Now I do not know who the men were or what they were discussing and I had no idea what would have happened if I had not been armed. All I know was that having my gun made a difference.

I have ensured that I carry it now always. And I hope the time never comes that I have to use it.

CHAPTER TWO

THE CASTLE DOCTRINE

The Castle Doctrine (also known as a "Castle Law" or a "Defense of Habitation Law") is a legal doctrine based on United Kingdom law. Principally, the Doctrine was based on the UK ruling that an Englishman's home is his Castle. And that he has a right to defend it based on that law. That used to be a cornerstone of English Law, sadly no longer is.

In America, that law designates one's place of residence (or, in some states, any place legally occupied, such as one's car or place of work) as a place in which one enjoys protection from illegal trespassing and violent attack. The Castle Doctrine then goes on to give a person the legal right to use deadly force to defend their place, and any other innocent persons legally inside it, from violent attack or an intrusion which may lead to violent attack.

In a legal context, therefore, use of deadly force which actually results in death may be defended as justifiable homicide under the Castle Doctrine.

As a result, in general, twenty-six states have adopted a Castle Doctrine, which includes Alaska, California, Colorado, Connecticut, Georgia, Hawaii, Illinois, Kansas, Maine, Maryland, Massachusetts, Michigan, Minnesota, Mississippi, Missouri, Nevada, New Jersey, North Carolina, North Dakota, Ohio [extends to vehicles of self and immediate family], Oregon, Pennsylvania, Rhode Island, Utah, West Virginia, and Wyoming.

However, each state differs with respect to the specific instances in which the Castle Doctrine can be invoked, and what degree of retreat or non-deadly resistance (if any) is required before deadly force can be used.

The law does allow a person who is attacked to defend oneself in most cases, however the use of force does not mean you have a license to kill. As I often tell my CCDW students, you are not James Bond.

Remember that the decision to shoot, or not is a split second one. In an ideal world you would have time to assess the situation weigh up the variables and decide how real the threat is. Unfortunately, most encounters happen so suddenly and unexpectedly that we do not have that luxury.

A home invader is most likely to break in at night or at least after dark. An armed intruder can kick open a door and rush into the house in around 3 to 6 seconds.

If your firearm is on your person or immediately accessible then you may have time to draw it and fire. You will have precious little time for much else. The encounter is over in moments. If you manage to fire and hit the intruder, then you may have stopped the attack, but your problems may only just be starting.

If the attacker is hit and dies, then you can expect to be arrested and taken into custody. This is standard police procedure. This does not mean the Police feel that you are guilty of murder or even assault. It takes a while to investigate a shooting, and the Police will take their time to gather all the evidence.

In some cases the evidence is clear cut and the intruder may have been carrying a gun or other weapon and there may be witnesses. The offender may be known to the police and have a record of similar activities. The Police would prefer to take you from the scene and interview you in the calm of an interview room.

Meanwhile other officers can photograph the scene, take measurements, and identify witnesses. Your gun will be taken and examined by forensics, and bullets fired that missed will be located, with the angle they were fired correlated to the account that you gave. Bullets taken from the body will also be examined as to type caliber, barrel grove marks, and any modifications.

Blood spatter and stains will be photographed and the deceased will also be meticulously photographed before being moved. Examination of clothing will reveal how close the victim was to the muzzle of the gun when shots were fired. Entry and exit wounds can also show how far the muzzle of the gun was from the victim. An autopsy will reveal if the deceased was still alive when the shots were fired. In short, the Police will gather enough evidence to decide if this incident matches the criteria for Castle Doctrine.

The wheels of justice move slowly but they do move, and if you are unlucky enough to find yourself in front of a court and jury, the trial will be lengthy and thorough.

What took 10 seconds on the night in the incident will be dissected and drawn out over several weeks. You will be asked why you felt so sure the intruder was a threat, what he said if anything, what you replied, how many shots did you fire, where did you aim, and so on.

To make a determination the police will have to decide if your use of deadly force was justified. You are allowed to fire at an attacker and continue to fire until they are no longer a threat. That means; if your first shot disables the assailant and leaves him in a collapsed state screaming in pain and casting aspersions on your parental status, you cannot shoot them again.

However, if they are continuing to threaten you and advancing on you with a weapon, then further shots are not only permitted, but in my opinion advisable.

It is a sobering fact that the majority of gunshot wounds are survivable, and are unlikely to stop the attacker instantly. Even point blank range head shots are not necessarily fatal as the courageous former Congresswoman Gabrielle Giffords can attest.

However, a deliberately aimed head shot could be construed as intention to kill. Again the circumstances of the incident will determine the actions taken.

So let us say that you have fired and the intruder is down, and obviously in pain. They need to be watched carefully while you dial 911.

Remember that the intruder is unlikely to be a middle aged ruffian with several days' growth of beard. They are more likely to be young men or women, maybe of the same age as your own son or daughter. There is likely to be an overwhelming regret of having caused the injury to them and an understandable desire to try and undo the harm. This could be a fatal mistake for you.

You cannot tell if the wounded intruder is armed or how seriously they are injured. You can best help them by getting the police and paramedics to the scene ASAP.

Certainly, you can advise them to apply pressure to the wound and sit still. On no account should you approach them. Even if the intruder appears unconscious, all you are doing is giving them a chance to get ahold of your gun or get the upper hand.

Try to avoid speaking to the intruder or engaging them in conversation. Remember, intruders rarely operate alone and their friends may decide to come and see what happened. You must always be ready for another encounter, stay alert.

The emotional shock of using a firearm on another human being is one that can never be underestimated. It is probably true that your life will never quite be the same again.

You can expect that the parents and family of the person that you shot to be very hostile and even threatening towards you. However all of this must not be allowed to cloud your judgment. Your life and the lives of your family depend upon you making the right decision and you must not falter in protecting them.

Now with that knowledge let us revisit the Home invasion scenario that introduced this book.

Debbie did a number of things right and other things so wrong that they cancelled out the good, and left her at the mercy of her attacker.

To outsmart a criminal, then it is necessary to think like one.

Cutting the phone line to the house will impede any attempt to call for assistance.

A few minutes observing outside, showed our criminal that Debbie had retired to bed. He had observed her locking the doors. A single light on in the bed room showed him which room she was in.

Debbie's concern for her children's safety was commendable, but misguided. Keeping the gun in the gun safe, even after they were asleep meant that she would need to access it in a hurry. Ask yourself; how long does it take you to wake up, access the safe and open it, retrieve the gun and then bring it to bear on the attacker.

Now once the burglar kicks in the door they only need to run to Debbie's bedroom before she can get out of bed, open the safe, and grab her gun. Do the calculations yourself, if that is necessary. The intruder is already in the house, awake, alert, and their adrenaline is already pumping.

Debbie left her cell phone on charge in the kitchen. Out of her immediate reach once the intruder came in. She turned on her light, showing the intruder exactly where she was.

Having a firearm for protection is, in itself, not enough. The gun needs to be immediately accessible and loaded. In short you need to develop a plan. When possible, contacting the police should be you first priority.

My recommendation would be to call them as soon as you are aware of a break-in occurring. Always use 911, and always give your address first. The knowledge that the police are on their way will have a positive effect on your actions. But what if you have to shoot? That is what we will explore next.

CHAPTER THREE

JUSTIFICATION OF THE USE OF DEADLY FORCE

Every State in the USA recognizes the right to self-defense. However there are wide variations on the legal use of such force depending upon which State you reside in.

Generally there has to be a direct threat of attack and the use of deadly force is necessary to prevent serious injury or death to yourself, family or other person. And you should also remember that just because you have the right to use deadly force that does not mean you have to do so.

If the threat stops then so does the right to use deadly force. This was clearly illustrated in the much cited case of People v Couch.

This case centered on an incident in 1990 when a fleeing felon was shot by an armed citizen in order to prevent his escape. The Michigan Supreme Court ruled that Archie L. Couch did not have the right to use deadly force against the suspected felon because the suspect did not pose a threat of injury or death to Couch. This is an important distinction.

This fact was enforced by a far more recent case that sparked a media blitz between second amendment supporters and anti-gun groups.

As usual the Police were caught in the middle and the courts finally settled the case.

In May 1990, 59 year old Jerome Ersland was in his pharmacy when two masked youths entered the premises. Sixteen Year old Antwun Parker was accompanied by 14 year old Jevontai Ingram who was holding a gun.

Ersland had been robbed a number of times in the past and kept two pistols in the pharmacy. He produced one from under the counter and fire one shot at Parker. The bullet hit parker in the head and he collapsed onto the floor. Ingram turned and fled the building, and Ersland pursued him, emptying his gun at the fleeing robber. He missed.

Ersland then returned to the Pharmacy. Parker lay where he fell, still alive but in a deep coma. Ersland then put down his empty gun and went to a drawer where he kept the second gun. He walked over to Parker and fired 5 more rounds at point blank range into the teenager's body.

He then called 911 and informed the Police. The Pharmacist told the Police that he had shot Parker again as he was trying to sit up and he feared that he still represented a threat.

The story was quickly disproved when forensic and pathological examination showed that the teenager could not have moved his head. Injury had caused pressure on the brain that rendered him unconscious.

Jerome then changed his story saying
that both robbers had guns, and that
he himself was suffering from PDSD
following combat missions in Iraq and
Afghanistan. He showed an injury to
his arm and stated he had been
wounded in the incident.

The fact was that Ersland had never
served in combat or been deployed to
any war zones.

No shots were ever fired by Ingram.
This was verified by the security
footage. The injury was a crude
attempt to bolster a crumbling story.
It was obviously self-inflicted and
medics quickly determined it was not
a gunshot wound. The jury took less
than 4 hours to convict Ersland and he
was sentenced to life imprisonment.

Ingram was also arrested and received the same sentence, as were two drivers of the getaway car, and the mastermind who employed the luckless teenagers.

The 4 were all convicted of first degree murder. The reason is that an Oklahoma law states that if a murder occurs during the commission of a felony, then all parties to that felony are equally guilty of that murder.

Ersland has appealed his sentence several times and has failed. Ingram was a juvenile, and had his case reviewed when he was 18 and was released on (parole) license. This case has illustrated the passions aroused on both sides of the self-defense debate.

A tour of the internet will show many ill-informed comments on the guilt or innocence of Ersland. It also shows the basic lack of understanding of the limits of self-defense in law. Clearly, you cannot pump bullets into an unconscious 16 year old and then claim you feared for your life due to the threat he posed.

Clearly, the unconscious youth presented no threat to Ersland. Ersland was armed and chose to shoot the unarmed youth as opposed to the armed one. Once Ingram had fled he also presented no threat, therefore for Ersland to pursue was also unjustified.

Carrying a gun for personal defense confers on you a serious responsibility, both mentally and morally.

In my judgment, the Jury got this one absolutely right. Ersland is guilty of Murder; and will get no sympathy for those of us who carry and use our guns purely as a last resort.

No chapter on justification would be complete without reference to the George Zimmerman case. As many of you will know this involved the shooting of a young black youth Trayvon Martin by a young Hispanic man George Zimmerman. Not since the O. J. Simpson case has a killing created so much of a media storm.

Unprecedented intervention in the case from the Justice Department and even the President of the United States muddied the waters. The media pressed the racial aspects of the shooting. The case, unfortunately for them, did not involve a black man being killed by a white man, so the media simply invented a new term white Hispanic.

In this digital age, 911 tapes were released and seized upon by both sides and small edited versions were put out to support each side's case. More seriously, some news organizations selectively edited some tapes to introduce a racial motive.

The Justice department moved quickly to take over the investigation and charge Zimmerman with murder long before any forensics and evidence had been fully gathered. It was one of the worst extremes of political interference in a case we have seen in this country.

Faced with such a smokescreen it is amazing that the truth was not lost or suppressed. It was certainly not for the want of trying. So what were the actual facts of the case, as determined by the police and forensic teams, and excluding all of the political spin and frenzied emotion?

George Zimmerman was a resident of a gated community in Florida and also a neighborhood watch volunteer.

This volunteer work involved watching for suspicious activity and reporting any such activity to the police. On the evening in question Zimmerman left is home to pick up some groceries from the store. It was raining and he was not on any sort of patrol. He was however armed and had a concealed carry permit issued by the State of Florida. The gun he carried was in a belt holster on his hip.

While returning from the store his attention was drawn to a young black male wearing a hoodie who appeared to be hanging around the gated housing area. This was suspicious, as he knew most of the residents, but did not recognize this young man. He stopped his vehicle and continued to observe the youth.

Zimmerman was aware of the high number of break-ins in the area, and also knew that all of them had been committed by young black males. The press later dubbed this as racial profiling.

Remember that Zimmerman was not a cop, and had no power to arrest suspects.

The youth caught sight of Zimmerman and moved away back into the gated community, out of sight. Zimmerman parked his vehicle and followed. He called the incident in and spoke to the dispatcher, giving him details and a description. The dispatcher asked if Zimmerman was following the youth and when he confirmed that he was, told him, OK, we don't need you to do that.

At this point Zimmerman states he turned around and headed back to his car to meet up with the officer being dispatched. There is no evidence to say when or if he turned around. The responding officers reached the scene and heard a gunshot. Quickly they located Zimmerman who was with the youth, who was lying on his back with a gunshot wound to the chest.

Zimmerman told the officer that he had been forced to shoot the youth in self-defense. The youth was pronounced dead and the police investigation commenced.

Zimmerman was bleeding from superficial cuts on the back of his head.

He was taken into custody and treated in the back of the police cruiser before being conveyed to the police station. His gun was seized for forensic analysis.

Initial enquires showed that a number of witnesses had called in, reporting a struggle between two men.

Although lighting was not good, the witnesses could make out one man straddling another and one was calling for help. None of the witnesses were able to identify the two men but did note their distinctive clothing; saying the man on top had a grey hoodie and the man underneath a red jacket.

When arrested, Zimmerman was wearing a red anorak.

The dead youth was dressed in blue jeans and a grey hooded sweatshirt.

Zimmerman's account was that he was jumped by Martin while on his way back to the car. Martin straddled him and began banging his head repeatedly against a concrete curbstone. Unable to free himself, Zimmerman had reached for his gun and the move was seen by Martin, who also tried to grab the gun. Zimmerman stated that he fired one shot from the hip upwards into Martins body.

Later, both Zimmerman's and Martins parents testified that the voice screaming for help was their son.

There were of course, no witnesses to the actual events.

The Police weighed up the evidence that showed consistencies with Zimmerman's account. He was released on bail pending further enquiries.

At this time the Department of Justice senior prosecutor arrived in Florida and took over the case. The Police chief in charge of the investigation resigned and the press were given free rein to say what they wanted and report any facts they wished, true or not.

The Police meanwhile, despite intense political pressure, continued with the investigations. Statements were taken and experts were called in to examine the evidence and test Zimmerman's account.

The media began a massive witch hunt on Zimmerman and his wife, releasing their address and details and forcing them into hiding. Local black power groups placed a bounty on his head.

Eventually the case came to trial and the evidence was presented to the Jury. Both defense and prosecution teams did their job as thoroughly as possible. But the evidence against Zimmerman quickly collapsed.

Expert witnesses testified that the injuries to Zimmerman were consistent with his account. Grass samples at the scene and on Zimmerman's clothing matched.

A ballistics expert testified that the fatal shot was fired with the muzzle of the gun in contact with the clothing about 2 to 3 inches from Martins body. This is a fact that could only have happened if Martin had been leaning over his victim allowing the hoodie to hang clear of the chest.

Florida has the same self-defense laws as most of the country. Deadly force is only permitted if you feel your life is threatened. Zimmerman had contended that he was in imminent danger of death or being seriously injured, as a result of his head being pounded against the curbstone. The Jury agreed and acquitted him; in my opinion, the only verdict possible.

However, Zimmerman paid dearly for his actions that night.

It cost him his marriage and vilified him; thanks to the actions of a misinformed public and a media driven frenzy that should have had no place in modern Justice. No doubt the Zimmerman case will continue to be cited in many cases and books in the future.

A police photo of the scene shows Martins body and the poor lighting at the time.

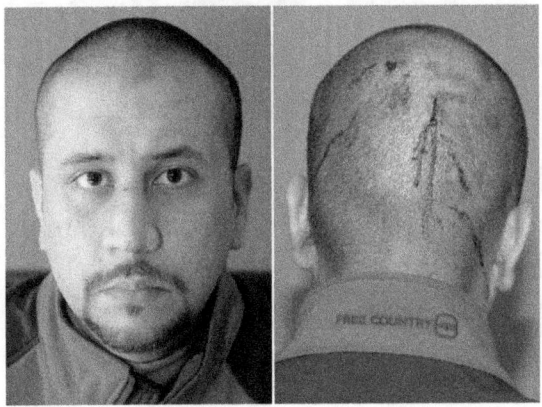

Police Photo of Zimmerman showing
injuries to his head.

Trayvon Martins' Selfie from his cellphone shows a different face than that portrayed by the media which used a 5 year old high school picture.

If all this makes you worried about carrying a gun for self-defense, then that is understandable. You may consider it too much of a gamble. But remember, like the young girl at the start of the book.

If you decide against arming yourself you are also gambling; this time with your life and the lives of your family.

The two cases above are extreme; there are countless stories of law abiding citizens using their guns for personal defense and never having had to face a court. If you take a professional firearms course and study the self-defense laws in your State then you should prevail.

Most armed citizens go through life without ever having to use a gun in personal defense. Still fewer have to actually fire the gun, and even fewer end up killing their attacker. Most Courts will give some leeway on the question of justifiable force.

For instance, in Kentucky if you had a reasonable fear of attack and you shot your attacker, even if you were mistaken and misinterpreted his actions, the law says you have a self-protection defense. The question is always;

"Was it reasonable under the circumstances to react with deadly force?" If the police are unsure they may refer the case to a Grand Jury to decide on an indictment. Even if you are totally justified in using deadly force, you may still be charged with some other related felony, such as wanton endangerment or assault. As I have said, all States have different laws.

I would urge all gun owners who carry a firearm for personal defense to obtain legal insurance. There are a number of organizations such as the USCCA and the Legal Action Defense Network that offer plans that will provide you with specialized legal counsel in the event of you being involved in a deadly force encounter.

As a Police Officer in the UK, I was required to read an accused person their rights after arresting them. These were similar to the US 'Miranda Rights' and had the same effect. It was always more difficult for me if an accused refused to answer any questions, because I was forced to rely on other evidence to investigate the case.

Most UK Attorneys would advise their clients to say nothing and let us prove the case. This was frustrating and often led to more work on my part. More importantly, it also often led to innocent persons being charged and put before a Court who had a good case or alibi but only revealed it in Court. This in turn led Magistrates and the Jury to ask why it was only now that the evidence turned up, and leading to a suspicion of fabrication.

In our concealed carry classes, we teach what is known as the Ayoob 5 point check list. This enables an accused person to give basic information to the attending police officer, without compromising their Miranda Rights. The Author Massad Ayoob has a background in Law enforcement and firearms law.

Basically, he states that you should identify yourself as the victim who was attacked. You should give brief details of yourself, name and address and show them your ID. Give the Officer a brief account of what happened. For example;

"I was asleep when this man broke in through my back door. I called 911 and grabbed my gun. As he burst into the bedroom I fired 3 shots and he fell there. I felt I had to defend myself. I am willing to sign a complaint."

Once that information is given, the officer will then have the basic picture of the incident. He will check the broken back door and note the time.

If you are questioned further, I would politely say that I will not answer any more questions until I have an attorney present. We will explore the procedure on dealing with the Police in Chapter 5.

CHAPTER FOUR

SHOT -

DOES NOT MEAN DEAD

Ok, so you have bought your gun and have been to a local training school and learned how to use it. The gun is kept in your bedroom at night and in your bag or holster during the day. You feel much safer.

You have not thought too much about having to use it but you know you are a fair shot and received praise from your instructor. You know the legal limitations of when you can and cannot shoot.

At any rate, you feel it is likely that the sight of a gun will scare off any intruder that is stupid enough to break in. You have not really considered what would happen if you get shot in the encounter. If asked, you may say something like;

'Well if I am to die then I'll take him/her with me.'

I have heard similar comments from students attending my courses. One question that I ask at every concealed carry class that I teach is;

"If you are shot, and you realize you have been shot, at that precise moment you realize something else. What is that?"

Usually only 20% of the class has the correct answer.

If you know you have been shot, then it is immediately apparent that you are not dead. There is of course a possibility that you may die, but you are alive at the moment, and can do something about it.

Let us go back to a suburb of Los Angeles in the year 1990. On June 9th to be precise, a young woman is driving her 1988 Ford Bronco SUV, she is returning to her home in Canyon County from a softball match.

Stacy Lim is a 27 year old officer in the LAPD. She has just completed her probationary training, having been a police officer for a little over 2 years. She was being followed. A dark SUV with 5 black occupants is behind her. Stacey notices the vehicle but takes no action.

Inside the car following her are 4 young men and a 14 year old girl, members of one of the Los Angeles gangs. They are not interested in the driver but do like her vehicle. Stacey is not wearing a uniform, and to the gang she appears to be just another dumb woman that will provide them with a set of wheels. One of the young boys had stolen his mother's .357 magnum revolver and now clutched it firmly.

Stacey pulled into her driveway and gathered up her kit, stuffing it into her bag. The last thing she did before exiting the vehicle was pick up her police issue handgun, intending to tuck it under her arm but changed her mind when confronted with one of the SUVs occupants.

A 15 year old male gang member was pointing a revolver at her chest and demanded that she hand over the keys to her 2 year old Bronco.

Stacey immediately dropped her bag, leveled her own gun at the gunman and yelled, "Police Officer drop the gun." She had barely completed the sentence, and the boy when shocked by it, fired.

The bullet, a hollow-tipped magnum load, fragmented and nicked nearly every organ in her torso; her stomach, her intestines, her liver. It shattered her spleen, cracked a rib, and put a hole in the base of her heart before exiting out her back leaving a large exit wound.

"The only thing it missed was her lung and kidney," she said. Later she added that the bullet felt like a hot Javelin searing through her body.

Stacey was staggered by the impact. The youth ran towards the back of the car and then turned and leveled the gun again. Stacey fired first and she did not miss. Three shots in quick succession struck the boys chest and he fell back firing his gun repeatedly and harmlessly into the air. He landed on the driveway where he died.

Stacey scanned the area, but the other gang members had gone. She turned toward the house but only made it as far as the bottom of her drive before collapsing.

Her last act before losing consciousness was to eject her magazine and throw it into the bushes. Her police training had taught her to never leave a gun and ammunition for a bad guy. The other assailants fled the scene leaving behind the dead boy and a young 14 year old girl hiding in the bushes. The crying and scared girlfriend of the dead boy was still there when law enforcement arrived. She supplied the names of the assailants and they were quickly rounded up.

The responding officers found Stacey where she fell. Despite their efforts, her pulse weakened and she stopped breathing, a condition known to the medics as Flatline.

The medics persevered and shocked
her back to life. She was rushed to
the hospital, her chances looked slim.

After two hours of surgery at Henry
Mayo Newhall Hospital, Stacey was
on life support. While in intensive
care, she went Flatline again.

The doctors informed her family that
she was losing too much blood and
that they would have to get her back
into surgery. They opened her chest a
second time and spent 45 minutes
massaging the heart back to life. It
worked, but she was not out of the
woods yet.

Doctors also found a severed artery
that runs along a rib in her back and
worked to repair it.

But despite their efforts, their outlook for Lim's recovery was bleak.

Finally the doctors told her family, "She's got about an hour and half to two hours left to live. The only thing keeping her alive is machines, so do what you need to do to prepare yourselves."

A nurse asked Lim's younger brother to sign donor cards and authorize the removal of her undamaged organs once she died. It appeared the police department already had written her obituary. It seemed that everyone had written Lim off.

But miraculously, Stacey survived and astounded both her doctors and the department.

She remained in a coma for a week
before opening her eyes. Stacey Lim
is a living legend in her department.

On Thursday May 10th 2012 LAPD
Chief Charlie Beck awarded Stacey
the Purple Heart at a ceremony in LAs
Grand Ballroom.

Officer Stacey Lim at the award
ceremony in 2012

The same living legend description
can be applied to another police
officer Deputy Jennifer Fulford.

~ 85 ~

Deputy's Jennifer Fulford and Jason Gainor were attached to the Orange County Florida Sheriff's Department. On May 5th 2004 she and her partner Jason were working the day shift when shortly before 0800 a call went out:

"Suspicious circumstances at a residence. An 8 year old informant had told the 911 operator that "strange men" were inside his Medford Court residence in the Pine Hills district of Orlando. The eight-year-old boy was whispering and his cell phone connection was poor. The dispatcher had been unable to get any other details. Two other, Deputies, Dwayne Martin, and Kevin Curry responded to the call, Fulford and Gainor were sent as back up.

~ 86 ~

When Fulford and Gainor arrived at the address, they found Deputies Martin and Curry already on scene and speaking with the informant's mother in the driveway. The child informant was nowhere to be seen. As Jenny got out of the car a nervous woman approached her and said,

"There are three men in my house. I don't know who they are or what they want."

Despite Jenny's best efforts the woman refused to elaborate, but added that her children were seated inside a van parked in the garage.

Curry and Martin directed the mother to wait on the opposite side of the street while a helicopter and a K-9 deputy were requested to respond.

The two deputies then took up surveillance postures on opposite sides of the property. Deputy Fulford then approached the house.

Small time crook John Dzibinski was always looking for an easy buck. Now, he'd been tipped off to a large amount of marijuana and cash stashed inside a residence in suburban Orlando. Dzibinski's source had told him the house was "easy pickings." The husband was out of town, leaving just the wife and three young children at the property. This should be like taking candy from a baby. Dzibinski had invited two drug gang members, George Jenkins and Shaun Byrom, to accompany him for an easy score. Like Dzibinski, Jenkins had an extensive criminal record.

One of the offences on his record was home invasion and robbery. Normally the trio armed themselves with AK47s when on a drug hit but for this job they figured they only needed their handguns.

At first it had gone well, but now things were going wrong. Police officers were outside talking to the mother of the woman who they currently held at gunpoint. They ordered her to go out and get rid of the cops. They watched nervously from behind the curtains as she approached the officers, but they did not leave. They saw one female officer start to walk towards the house. Panic began to set in.

Jenny Fulford was 31 years old and was due to be married and had already bought the dress she would wear on the big day. As she approached the open garage door she could see nothing amiss, but something was not right. It was clear the woman was hiding something. She could clearly see a van and an SUV parked inside. Entering the garage on the driver's side of the van, she peered into the van's windows. Two small children were buckled into car seats staring up at her. There was no sign of the third child.

She smiled comfortingly at the two kids, and then tried the doors. They were both locked but the kids seemed unharmed so she began to back out from the garage.

As she did so, she saw that Deputy Martin had moved forward onto the driveway taking up a position just outside the garage entrance. "I can't get the kids out," she said, and started toward him. "The doors are..."

She didn't get a chance to finish the sentence. There were male voices, fast, agitated voices. They were coming from the opposite side of the minivan. Jenny turned towards the sound. Without warning, a volley of three to four shots rang out.

Fulford reacted instinctively dropping to the ground, she keyed her mic attached to her lapel and advised "Shots fired!"

Deputy Martin had been hit in the shoulder by that first burst of gunfire.

He rolled out of the line of fire drawing his sidearm as he made for cover.

Unable now to see Martin, who had moved out of the line of sight, Fulford drew her Glock and spun around to face the gun welding attacker. His shots were coming from the back of the van. Fulford braced herself just as the six-foot figure of Jenkins emerged from the rear of the minivan, his 9mm semi auto pistol blazing. His target was Jenny, who was bringing her own gun to bear. As bullets slammed into her body, undaunted, the officer returned fire. Jenkins collapsed to the ground against the garage wall badly wounded but still firing. Fulford ducked down behind the wheel well of the minivan. Movement toward the front of the vehicle caught her eye.

John Dzibinski had entered the garage and was now also firing at her.

Gunfire surrounded the injured young officer. Jenkins was firing, Dzibinski was firing, Deputy Martin was firing, and of course, she was firing. Now on the garage floor, Jenny was trapped between the minivan and an SUV and exchanging fire with suspects to her front and rear. At least with Jenkins at the rear she'd been able to get cover behind the van. But with Dzibinski now at the front, leaning over the hood of the van and shooting, the brave young girl had nowhere to go.

Trapped against the wall, she alternated her fire back and forth, consciously using her Glock and its .45 caliber Speer hollow points to both suppress the fire of her attackers and stop their attacks. She had practiced this tactic many times on the range, now she had to put it into use. Her life depended on it.

Dzibinski left the front of the van and ducked behind cover. For the first time, Jenny took stock of her injuries. She'd taken several rounds in her legs. Bleeding and in pain she prepared to reengage in the battle.

Dzibinski stood up firing. Fulford took aim, and with a well-placed volley of shots that was zeroed in on his exposed upper torso her target collapsed before her gun ran dry.

~ 94 ~

Performing a textbook tactical reload she immediately encountered a second volley of shots from Jenkins who was firing from the rear of the van. One of Jenkins' rounds slammed into Fulford's dominant arm, but not before she fired a round that caught him center mass and put him down and out of the fight.

Her right arm was no longer functional. Fulford transferred her weapon to her left hand and pivoted in the direction of where she had last seen the second suspect.

Dzibinski leaned out from the corner of the van and again fired. Fulford returned fire. Dzibinski was making the most of his cover. But Fulford was dialed in.

A round caught the drug dealer in the head, and he fell back out of her view he would never get up. The gunfight was over. Blood streamed down Fulford's wounded right arm and formed a pool on the floor. Her vision blurred and the room began a slow spin. She could feel herself starting to black out. She fought to stay conscious.

Suddenly, Fulford heard Dep. Curry shouting her name and asking if she was OK. Fulford shook her head "No." Curry and Gainor hurried into the garage and carried her out to the street.

Fulford was transported to Orlando Regional Medical Center. At the hospital, Fulford grabbed the arm of her boss Sheriff Kevin Beary.

"Tell the range instructors they were right," she told Beary. "And tell them thanks. Everything they taught me about tactics and survival mindset came to me when I most needed it."

Fulford spent two days being treated for her injuries before recuperating at home.

Dzibinski's shots had hit her right knee, left ankle, left thigh, and left buttock. Jenkins' rounds had caught her in the right forearm, right shoulder, and left pinky finger. Her body had absorbed a total of seven bullets. Her attackers were not so lucky Jenkins was pronounced dead at the scene. Dzibinski was transported to a local hospital where he was pronounced brain-dead prior to being taking off life-support a week later.

The third suspect, Byrom, surrendered after the gunfight and is now serving life in prison.

Officer Jenny Fulford made a full recovery. She is now married and back on the job working as a detective with the Orange County Sheriff's Office child abuse detail.

Orange County Deputy Jennifer Fulford

T
he blood spattered garage floor where Deputy Fulford shot it out with 2 armed drug dealers

a
bove, the front of the residence in Pine Hills.

Surviving armed encounters are not just the prerogative of law enforcement. There are numerous cases of homeowners and other armed citizens using their guns to defend themselves, even when they are shot while doing so.

Take the case of 28 year old Kenny Davis, in Tennessee.
On October 24th 2012 Kenny's older brother Dareese Lee and their mother Sara Lee were at their home on Bigelow Street, in Frayser, Tennessee. It was close to midnight when Dareese answered a knock at the door. Outside were 3 armed men who pushed their way into the house. They were not wearing masks, and ordered Dareese to the floor.

They kept demanding, "Where is it" over and over. Kenny was in the back of the house, and hearing the commotion grabbed his own gun and ran to investigate. The gunmen, upon seeing Kenny opened fire striking him in the neck and lower abdomen.

Despite his wounds Kenny returned fire hitting one of the gunmen in the head killing him instantly, the other intruders fled. Despite his wounds Kenny made it to a neighbor's house.

Joshua Boswick, a friend of the neighbor began to apply first aid while the neighbor called 911. He cut off Davis' shirt and applied pressure to the wounds.

Twenty Eight year old Kenny Davis had been shot twice, but in returning fire his cowardly assailants ran. In the next chapter we will explore in depth the mental issues of an armed encounter.

CHAPTER FIVE

DEALING WITH THE POLICE

"Speak softly and carry a big stick! You will go far."

President Theodore Roosevelt

One question that frequently crops up in a self-defense shooting is what I can expect when the Police arrive. Remember, that firstly you are not the criminal here; you will initially be in a State of shock, and depending on the condition of the 'shot' intruder.

Your reaction will be retreat from the scene or stay with the downed suspect. If the suspect is incapacitated he may not be able to pursue you but could still represent a threat. He needs to be monitored. The response time of the Police will depend upon a number of factors.

Police officers will be tasked to attend an incident in order of priority. The first contact you will make when calling 911 is the Police Dispatcher. This is not necessarily a Police Officer, and in fact is more likely to be a civilian operator who is trained in dealing with the general public and in categorizing an incident. It is therefore very important that you give her/him the information needed to get you Police assistance quickly.

You should pause momentarily to gather your thoughts. If you blurt out that you've shot someone and need help, you are already in trouble. The dispatcher will probably ask you to repeat what you said, and then ask a number of questions that you may think stupid and irrelevant. Such as, 'can I have you name please and your address.'

If you are prepared you should say something to the effect of;

"Hello this is Jane Smith of *address & City*. An intruder has just broken into my home and I was forced to shoot him to protect myself."

The dispatcher instantly knows who is calling, where you are and can see the information given matches the details on their screen from the 911 system.

She will tell you to stay on the line while she contacts the nearest police unit. At this time your call is being recorded. Anything you say or the dispatcher says will become evidence in any subsequent legal action.

The dispatcher will pass details to the responding unit. Tell them your description and where you are at your location.

For Example;

'I am upstairs in my bedroom. I am wearing a dressing gown and have blonde hair.'

Ask that this information be conveyed to the attending officer. Expect the dispatcher to ask you further questions.

Remember that it is not unreasonable for them to ask, but keep any questions and answers regarding you or the perpetrators actions short and concise at this stage. Remember your comments are being recorded.

A good dispatcher will not question you about the incident but will enquire if you are injured and if anyone else is in the house. These are questions that the attending officer(s) need to know.

When the officer(s) arrive, the dispatcher will tell you they are outside. You may or may not know this depending upon the location of your safe room/bedroom that you are making a stand in. At this stage you do not know for sure if the intruder is alone.

If you hear a noise downstairs and the dispatcher has not told you of the police arrival, then tell her. They will confirm if the police are at the address and inside or not. If they are not then, there is a possibility that there is more than one intruder is in the house. This information must be immediately conveyed to the dispatcher. On no account leave your position to investigate the noise.

Once you have confirmed that the police are at the house, or on the property then you need to ensure they get to you as soon as possible. If possible, make yourself visible to the officers, but never do so holding your gun. It may be possible to throw a set of keys to the officer if you are upstairs or give them to him through the window if on the ground floor.

I must again stress that it is of the upmost importance that you do not have your gun in a position that could be perceived as a threat. It should be holstered if possible or placed in a pocket. You could be mistaken for the intruder if you are holding the gun. Obey all the instructions given to you by the attending officer. Their job is to secure the scene and confirm there is no further threat. The officers will take your gun, it is now evidence.

At this stage the condition of the intruder will be checked. If they are apparently dead, then the coroner will be contacted and the police will have to await his arrival before they can confirm this is a homicide.

The police will not usually leave you at the scene. They will probably detain you and maybe even arrest you.

On the other hand they may just ask you informally to attend the police station for an interview.

I would advise that you do not answer any questions other than a simple account of the incident.

Tell the officer that you understand how serious the situation is but that you do not wish to answer any further questions without an attorney being present.

It is important to remember, that after such an incident you will be in shock and will be in no condition to give an accurate and lucid account of what happened. Police Officers involved in shootings are not treated any differently.

Their guns are taken for evidence and they will also refuse to answer questions without their legal representative in attendance. The Police will therefore understand your stance.

As to how the Police will react, that is a different matter, and each State has a different take on armed citizens. Despite what you may hear on TV and in the media, most rank and file police officers are not against the lawful use of guns for self-defense purposes, even in a totally anti-gun State such as New York. This was evidenced by over 90% of the sheriffs in the state joining a law suit opposing the States Governor's arbitrary and draconian restrictions on handguns contained in the absurdly named SAFE Act.

The Police as previously stated do not have a legal duty to protect the US Citizen. Overall the police will be suspicious and wary when they arrive.

I recall when I was in training as a rookie cop in England; I asked if we could not show a little compassion and understanding, in some cases. My Instructor's reply was uncompromising.

"Compassion! You are a Nasty Suspicious evil minded Copper Challis, never forget that."

Well, I hope that during my long Police Career I never totally lost compassion. But I always took things as I found them and never jumped to conclusions.

A US police Officer knows he is more likely to face an armed encounter than his British Counterpart, though that is changing.

I fully expect the attending Officer at an armed encounter to approach warily with his sidearm drawn. You must see the situation from their perspective.

Also remember that some police Chiefs may not appear as pro-gun as their officers. This can be partly explained by the system in the US that has some senior Police officers elected as opposed to being selected on proven ability. If you are an elected commissioner of a large American city then you are probably tied to one of the main political parties and the City Mayor is also a member of that party.

Quite simply, if the city passes ordinances that the Commissioner does not agree with there is little he can do other than resign. It is for that reason that in the UK Police Officers of any rank are prohibited from taking an active part in politics. Promotion from constable to senior rank is by merit only. And every police officer has to start as a constable.

This gives them a unique understanding of police work and how it is carried out. Now I have to clarify that I am not suggesting an elected Sheriff is in anyway corrupt or unable to do a good job. What I am alluding to is the perception of that Officer in the mind of a victim of crime.

An example may be a fervent NRA member of the Republican Party who has to report a break in to a County Sheriff who is a well-known left wing Liberal.

Now despite how fair and unbiased the Sheriff may be, the perception of the victim may be that it is pointless relying on him to investigate an incident where the victim had to shoot someone. This in turn may lead to vital evidence being overlooked due to non-cooperation from the victim. And the victims assumption, that the Sheriff will think he is hiding something if he refuses to answer questions. As we saw in the Zimmerman case, Politics has always played a part in Police Investigations but as we also saw in that case, the truth will always come out.

~ 115 ~

CHAPTER SIX

MINDSET

But after the fires and the wrath
But after searching and pain
His mercy opens us a path
To live with ourselves again

Rudyard Kipling
"The Choice"

Most armed citizens will go through
their lives without ever needing to use
a firearm.

Unless you are a combat veteran or a retired or serving police officer you will probably never have fired your weapon in anger, so to speak. In this chapter we will explore the psychological aspects of combat.

A combat veteran once described war as 90% boredom and 10% sheer terror. Although I served in the RAF as a mechanic in the early 70s I never saw combat and I can therefore not appreciate his statement.

I am therefore grateful to my good friend Lt Col Dave Grossman Retd, US Army, for his insight into what he calls the Bulletproof mind.

His books on the subject are required reading at the FBI academy and several major police Departments. He is considered to be one of Americas leading experts in this field. As a professor at west point he carried out research into a science that came to be called Killology.

So what is Killology? Basically it is the study on the effects of killing in battle and in other combat scenarios. Let us start with a somewhat startling fact.

Human Beings have a reluctance to kill other human beings. When given the choice, they would prefer to avoid it.

Another phenomenon known to the military is a condition known as battle crap. Basically this is a condition rarely seen in war films or documentaries. This is because it used to be associated with cowardice.

Battlecrap is quite simply the loss of bowel and bladder control before or during a battle.

Being physically sick or throwing up was also prevalent and again a stigma was attached. Until Col Grossmans team researched the condition no one had really studied it despite its history, going back to the roman occupation in Europe.

The problem with the cowardice theory was that that the soldiers suffering from it were also winning high awards for bravery. Clearly something was being missed.

The answer had nothing to do with the actual combat. It was a lesser known aspect of the body's natural defense mechanism.

Imagine you get home after a hard day and settle down to a well cooked meal. Following the meal you relax in front of the TV and put your feet up. After a while you close your eyes and the TV begins to fade. With your eyes closed and your hearing shutting down you quickly nod off.

Your family smile and say "well you're not as young as you used to be." You need your sleep, but they are wrong, as wrong as the assumption of cowardice of soldiers suffering from Battlecrap. Surprisingly there is a clear link.

The body requires approximately 80% of its energy output to digest food. Digestion can take from 4 to 6 hours depending on the size of the meal consumed.

Now a simplistic way of explaining the body defense mechanism is one that I use in class.

I am unashamedly a Star Trek fan. Imagine your body is the Enterprise. Your brain is Captain Kirk. Most episodes of that iconic series include an attack where the redoubtable Captain Kirk gives commands to divert all power to the forward shields, he may add; cut all non-essential systems. We must have more power.

OK let us leave the Enterprise and look at our own body dozing in front of the TV. The brain has diverted all available power to digestion.

It has closed down movement (You sat Down) Vision sensors (you closed your eyes) and communications (You fell asleep). Now your body can deal with the digestion and recharge your energy cells.

But say you are not able to rest, let us look now at the soldier, who has just finished a pre packed meal and is resting in his foxhole. Suddenly a mortar shell explodes nearby, enemy troops emerge from the woods ahead, and you grab your rifle and spring into action. Your adrenalin peaks as you engage the enemy, all your senses hearing, vision and movement are vital to your survival. Your body realizes that and immediately stops the digestion process, ejecting the consumed meal from whichever end it is nearest. It does so without warning.

So combat is stressful. That probably goes without saying, but stress is more than just worry, it can consume your psyche and drastically effect your decision making process, and that, in a combat situation can get you killed. This has been known by military commanders throughout the 20th century. More soldiers were pulled out of combat in WW1, WW2, and Korea than were killed by enemy action.

One of the major causes of stress is lack of sleep. We have all been asked by a doctor or friend at one time or another, "Are you getting enough sleep?"

In an effort to gather data on this subject The US army carried out a controlled experiment on an artillery battalion.

The Battalion was divided into 4 batteries and then was tasked with carrying out artillery exercises for 20 straight days every waking hour of every day.

The first battery group 1, seven hours of sleep each day Group 2, six hours Group 3, five hours and Group 4, four hours. Then their scores were compiled on a percentage of peak efficiency.

These are the accuracy results;

Group 1   98%

Group 2   50%

Group 3   28%

Group 4   15%

The results were startling and underlined the necessity for sleep.

We can all learn something from this study. Seven to eight hours of sleep per night is not only desirable it is essential. Police Officers know this, so does the military. Would you be happy to allow a doctor who had only 4 hours of sleep operate on you, knowing he was operating at around 15% of peak efficiency? And is it fair to you and your family to face an armed intruder with the same impediment?

So how do you prepare for such an encounter? Well first you will need to get the appropriate training in the operation and use of your firearm. Your local Police should be able to recommend a suitable trainer or shooting school.

The National Rifle Association will have lists of instructors in your State and area; their website is easily searchable and will give details of courses and costs.

Secondly you will need to get to know your weapon, its capabilities, and shortcomings. A gun dealer is not always the best person to ask advice from. Remember that they have a vested interest in selling you a gun and will usually push for the one that will give them a handsome return. This is in no way meant to criticize them; they are in Business to make a living.

I recently saw a blog post from a lady who was looking for a suitable gun for personal defense.

She posted this on a well-known firearms social media site and of course several instructors chipped in with advice. I did not do so but quickly rebuked an Instructor who suggested that she buy a Colt or Smith and Wesson handgun and forget about cheaper models. If she could not afford the $500 to $700 necessary then she would need to save up. What this instructor was saying in effect was that, if an intruder breaks into your home it is better to wave a receipt to show that you have put a deposit on a really bad ass gun, rather than point a .22 or .25 Raven pistol at him.

Despite extensive research I have never found a criminal who said they preferred to be shot with a smaller gun.

Being shot is not a pleasant experience and most intruders will turn tail and run when confronted with any gun.

When asked what gun Eva and I would recommend we always ask the circumstances of the would be purchaser. If they have been offered a gun or have already bought one then we will work to see that they get the best use out of the gun. Usually we have students who want to try out several guns. One person who had bought a shotgun because she was told you didn't need to aim it, got quite a wakeup call when we sent her to engage 5 targets set at various distances, all under 20 feet away.

The heavy recoil and unexpected misses unnerved her.

This was corrected with practice but had she had to fire the gun for the first time in a darkened bedroom with no ear protection at a rapidly moving target, the results could have been tragic. The shotgun is the most popular weapon for home defense as it has low penetration and a high fear factor. Defenders rarely have to fire the gun. However you need training just as much on the shotgun as the handgun.

Fear factor is of course a major consideration. As we have seen, most human beings are reluctant to kill other human beings. We would prefer for our opponent to run away rather than have to shoot them.

It is not true that you do not have to aim a shotgun, but the aim or sight picture does not have to be so precise.

This is because of the spread of shot from the gun expands as it leaves the barrel. However the expansion is not too much over; say the width of the average bedroom. If your aim is off by as much as a foot, the main charge could miss. However, the intruder that suddenly finds himself staring down the barrel of a shotgun is unlikely to wish to continue their attack. Unlikely, but not in every case.

If the intruder is heavily under the influence of drugs or drink, they may act differently and assume that you are too scared to shoot and that they will be able to disarm you without much trouble. If so, you must not hesitate to shoot. The first shot will not necessarily kill the attacker nor is it guaranteed to stop his attack.

It will depend on how close they are and where the shot strikes. In the movies, the blast of a shotgun results in the bad guy being thrown backwards with a force sufficient to propel him out of the house. In reality that will not happen. The effect of the gunshot will be immediate and very graphic. The intruder is likely to suffer sudden shock rendering him speechless for a moment and then leave him screaming and swearing on the floor. He may collapse and remain motionless on the floor. Either way you have stopped the attack. You must now call 911 and get help to your address. You cannot afford to engage the intruder in any conversation, or offer sympathy. You will need to keep a distance from them.

If they manage to run off, let them go,
and on no account try and follow.
That is not your concern. The threat
is over and you have survived. Now
comes the hard part.

CHAPTER SEVEN

PSYCOLOGY OF KILLING

"The best thing you can say to
someone going through a tragic loss is
not that,
"It's going to be alright"
It is:
"Hold on tight because this is going to
hurt like hell."
— John Passaro

Shortly before his death from a
Terrorist bomb in Sligo, Ireland in
August 1979, Retired British Military
commander, Statesman and uncle to
HRH Prince Charles, Lord Louis
Mountbatten of Burma, was
interviewed on TV.

The 78 year old statesman was asked about death and if he ever feared it. He replied that he did not really fear death, but his only hope was that when it did come it would be peaceful, in his bed surrounded by his family. It is a sentiment that many of us would share. However in the troubling times we live in today, violent death is everywhere.

Tragic though it is; death from road accidents or incurable disease is accepted as a fact of life. It is somehow different when death seems to have occurred without reason. Few of us have had to face someone intent on killing us, and have been forced to take the life of the person who does so.

In the last chapter we discussed the various physical and psychological effects of an armed encounter.

In the feature film '*Unforgiven*', Clint Eastwood's character made the following observation.

"It's a hell of a thing killing a man; you take away all he ever was and all he ever will be."

This is as true as it is profound. It is a fatal mistake to look at the man, or woman who is attacking you and think of things like, how old they are, why are they here, did they have a bad upbringing, are they married, do they have kids. Any such thoughts are certain to put your life at risk.

Soldiers often face such life and death situations.

In his excellent book 'On Killing', Lt Col Dave Grossman related the incident of a Special Forces officer in Vietnam who stormed an enemy position after taking fire.

"I got around the side and pointed my M16 at them and this person just turned around and stared, and I froze co's it was a boy. I would say between the ages of twelve and fourteen."

"When he turned at me and looked, all of a sudden he turned his whole body and pointed his automatic weapon at me. I just opened up. Fired the whole 20 rounds right at the kid. He just lay there. I dropped my weapon and cried."

This Green Beret was a battle hardened soldier who had faced death many times. His reaction to the death of this young boy soldier was understandable. Many soldiers in many wars have faced such decisions. Some have hesitated too long and paid the ultimate price. The average home defender will not be a battle hardened Green Beret, nor will the intruder be a middle aged career man with murder on their mind. It is more likely that the defender will be a housewife and/or mother, and the intruder a young teen male or female with no weapon. This of course changes the rules somewhat.

It has been known for years that killing at a distance is easier than killing up close.

I recall a Battle of Britain fighter pilot who said he shot down aircraft not people. It was easier to think of it that way. On one occasion, a German pilot who had bailed out came too close to his Hurricane, and as a result his parachute draped over its wing. The RAF pilot took great care to maneuver the aircraft so the German could slide free and resume his descent into captivity. Moments before this pilot had been desperately trying to kill him, now he was no longer a threat but a fellow aviator who was in danger.

Another case from the Battle of Britain featured a Luftwaffe fighter pilot who had just shot down a Spitfire.

He circled back and flew low over his victim, who was floating in his life jacket in the English Channel some miles from the shore. The German opened his cockpit and dropped his own life raft into the sea, gave a wave and flew back to France. An act that meant the German would have no raft if he ended up in the sea also. Such actions show us that even in the carnage of battle there is room for humanity.

The shock of shooting a human being is traumatic. Before each of our personal defense and Concealed carry classes I pass around an album showing gunshot victims. I do this to show the students the consequences of shooting another human being.

It is something they have to consider before carrying a firearm for self-defense.

This brings me to another fundamental truth. Human beings have a reluctance to kill other human beings. Military studies throughout history have shown this to be true. Of course there are exceptions such as the serial killers. In my previous book *'Compulsion to Kill', I* drew attention to the rise in violent video games, and its relation to the school shootings. However, these incidents are relatively rare. When you are face to face with someone and you have the power to end their life, then and there, the question is always; will you pull the trigger. Perhaps a better question should be; *"Do I have to kill this person?"*

In the highly recommended book 'Deadly Force Encounters', the authors Dr. Alexis Artwohl and Loren Christiansen listed 13 effects of combat. This list was compiled from surveys of 141 police offers who had been involved in a in an armed encounter (Gunfight). These are termed Perceptual Distortions in Combat.

1. Diminished 85%
2. Intensified Sound 16%
3. Tunnel Vision 80%
4. Automatic Pilot 74%
5. Heightened Visual Clarity 72%
6. Slow Motion Tune 65%
7. Temporary Paralysis 7%
8. Memory Loss for part of the event   51%

9. Memory Loss for some of your actions 47%
10. Disassociation 40%
11. Intrusive Distracting thoughts 26%
12. Memory Distortions 22%
13. Fast Motion Time 16%

A look at these observations will show a wide variation, all of us are different and therefore we react differently to any given situation. You will notice that at the top of the list is diminished sound. Well over three quarters of the interviewees reported this. Ask any Deer hunter to think back to the first deer they shot. Ask them if they recall hearing the shot, or feeling the recoil. Chances are they will not. Most Police Officers involved in sudden combat also report similar experiences.

Tunnel vision also scores high. Think of the bank robber who walks up to the teller, points a gun in their face, and says, "Hand over the money."

When questioned later by the police, they can give a detailed description of the gun, a revolver, and hollow point tips on the cartridges; maybe even describe the ring they were wearing on their trigger finger. Ask the teller to describe the robber however, and their replies will most likely be, average build average clothes, not too sure.

The reason is the terrified teller saw the gun, and only the gun, a classic case of tunnel vision. I attended a police lecture in 1975 while at the police training school in England. The lecture was on observations and eye witness testimony.

We were about 10 minutes into the lecture when a man suddenly burst into the room and fired six rounds at the sergeant from a revolver. The 'victim' collapsed over the podium. We sat in shocked silence, no one moved. The chief instructor then entered the classroom and announced.

"Right, you have all seen Sergeant Harvey here shot down in his prime. You all got a good look at his killer. Now I want all of you to write a clear statement with a full description of the killer."

We all complied and I felt confident. After we all finished the statements were collected and the descriptions read out. All gave a clear description of the gun, but the rest of the descriptions varied wildly.

Then the "Killer" re-entered the room and we saw what we had all missed.

He was wearing one large rubber boot and one slipper, a variety of brightly colored tops and several other very distinctive items of clothing. All of us had experienced Tunnel Vision. It was a sobering lesson that served me well during my career.

65% of the interviewees experience slow motion action. We have all seen the movies where the bad guy flies through the air and plate glass window in slow motion. Whilst this is usually done for effect, it actually happens in reality.

By that, I do not mean time actually slows down, but rather that your brain perceives it to do so.

I experienced it personally while watching a 50 lb. hatch cover blown off a cabin cruiser, rise up about 100 feet, and slowly tumble towards me in ultra-slow motion. I was saved from serious injury by a friend dragging me clear.

It is important to understand these anomalies as they are common in a high stress situation. Partial memory loss is also common. This is why it is important for you to take at least 24 hours to calm down and take stock of your emotions.

Once the proverbial gun smoke has cleared, you will experience another wide range of emotions. Surprisingly, first among these will be joy. Almost ecstasy. This is due to the realization that you have just survived a brush with death.

This is often followed by an overpowering feeling of guilt as you realize that you have possibly ended a life, you are facing trouble with the police, your friends, and slowly you begin to look at the consequences of what is in store. These are natural emotions, familiar to anyone who has served in combat. Extreme guilt is also a common emotion felt after combat.

The following account from a soldier who had killed his opponent at close range is telling and it is one you will not find in Hollywood.

"My experience was one of revulsion and disgust; I dropped my weapon and cried. There was so much blood ...I vomited and I cried. I felt remorse and shame.

"I can remember whispering "I'm sorry and then just throwing up."

On Killing (Back Bay Books)

Lt Col D Grossman

Of course all this may cause deep worry to the home defender, but that is not my intention. I am a firm believer in the old adage, fore warned is fore armed. It is important that these emotions are known and understood before the armed encounter.

As a young Police officer I was required to attend all autopsies for the first year of my service. Our Instructor had prepared us for this experience with a very graphic description of what takes place.

It certainly put me off my lunch, but when I attended my first autopsy I knew what to expect and dealt with the unpleasantness by asking the pathologist questions about the conclusions he was making.

Surprised that I had not turned green, he was happy to show me a rupture in a cranial blood vessel that had led to death. I survived that autopsy without fainting and have felt ever grateful to my trainer for preparing me for the experience. After my 1st year I made a point of volunteering to attend at least 1 per year, This ensured that I steeled myself to the blood and horror, and this in turn made me more prepared to deal with fatal accidents and death in my career.

What is important after a shooting is doing the right thing. Do not disturb any of the evidence. If you are on the phone to dispatch then do not speak too much, let the dispatcher talk to you and in the meantime sit down and breathe slowly and deeply, 10 to 15 breaths.

The increase in oxygen to your brain will do wonders for bringing you back from the near panic stage. It will be natural for you to discuss what happened with friends and your spouse, or parents. Remember that counseling is a recognized form of therapy.

Hopefully this chapter has given you an insight into the mindset of being in a deadly force encounter. Remember, this is not the movies, this is real life…

CHAPTER EIGHT
CHOICE OF FIREARM

The most frequent question asked by students is

"What gun should I get?"

Most are disappointed to hear that we do not recommend any particular firearm. This is because everyone is an individual. Choosing a firearm is as personal as buying a pair of shoes or boots. We believe that a gun should be comfortable in its user's hands and fit for purpose. You must feel comfortable holding and shooting it and also proficient with it in an emergency situation.

Statistics show us that the most common home defense firearm is a shotgun. There are many reasons for this and a lot of them can be laid at Hollywood's door. The shotgun has a high fear factor, and few people can fail to be alarmed at the sound of a pump action gun being racked. The sound is unmistakable.

It has a reputation as being always reliable and it doesn't need aiming.

Both of these are misconceptions. In fact, the shotgun in semi auto and pump action models can malfunction just as easily as its rifle counterpart.

If the shotgun is your choice of personal defense firearm, then you should be aware of some basic facts. Let us first look at what a shotgun is.

Basically, a shotgun has a smooth bore, which means there is no rifling (Lands and Grooves) cut into the inside of the barrel. Rifling is present in other firearms from small handguns to large military howitzers. Its purpose is to cause the bullet to rotate rapidly as it leaves the muzzle and this ensures the bullet will maintain a straight course to its target. Shotguns are close range weapons, and the shotgun shell normally does not contain just one bullet but many small pellets.

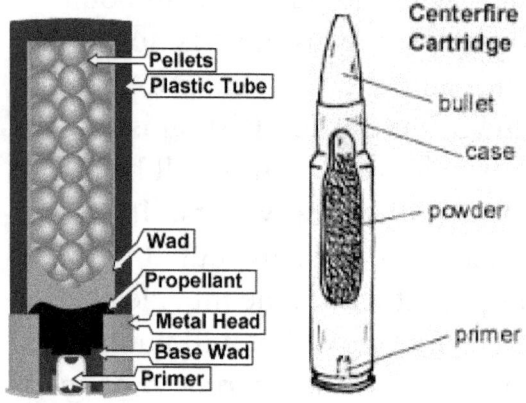

Pellets
Plastic Tube
Wad
Propellant
Metal Head
Base Wad
Primer

Centerfire Cartridge
bullet
case
powder
primer

<u>The shot shell (left) and the center fire cartridge (right) showing the different construction of each</u>

It is therefore unnecessary to have riflings in a shot gun. The illustration above shows the difference in construction between the two types of ammunition.

~ 154 ~

Most shotguns have a choked barrel. This means they taper from the breach to the muzzle end. The reason is to compress the shot into a tight package before it leaves the muzzle. The shot is contained in a plastic cup called a wad. Once free the cup opens out and the package of shot continues towards the target, expanding as it travels. Each small pellet will penetrate its target and the result is called the shot pattern. Each gauge of shotgun will produce a different pattern. The tighter the choke the tighter the pattern will be.

Hunters will test their shotguns by firing at a sheet of paper and measuring the radius of the shot pattern. This is important if your target is a turkey or pheasant flying away from you.

Most 12 gauge shotguns have an effective range of around 35 yards. After which the shot pattern is too wide to be effective. However when used within the home, the shot pattern is reduced to a few inches. The effect is devastating on the human body at a range of 5 to 8 feet when the shot pattern is no more than 6 to 8 inches wide. This also shows how wrong the assumption is that you do not have to aim a shotgun. In a home defense situation, being 12 inches off could be enough to miss the target entirely.

If a shotgun is your choice of defense weapon, you should know your shot pattern.

In addition, there are a number of handguns now manufactured that will take shotgun ammunition.

Guns such as the Taurus 'Judge' and Smith and Wesson's 'Defender' models are capable of firing both. 410 shot shells and .45 long colt ammunition. The shot pattern of a 410 is far less than that produced by a 12 gauge shotgun and it should only be considered as a short range (10 feet or less) when used against a human target.

I recently patterned a Taurus judge at 21 feet and the shot pattern was around 5 feet wide. The concentration of shot pellets in the center (Kill) zone was less than 4. This would not have been sufficient to deter a threat. At 10 feet the 8 inch shot pattern was effective.

Handgun manufactures are aware of this and have produced small single shot derringer type handguns chambered in 12 gauge.

These too have disadvantages, notably the recoil, and the restriction of just one round.

Overall the 410 revolver is a good choice. As with most handguns, the longer the barrel is the more accurate the gun. A 'Judge' with a 5 inch barrel will inevitably produce a tighter shot pattern than a 2 or 3 inch barrel.

Pump action and semi auto shotguns are popular because of the fear factor and the stopping power at close range. However, they are usually more unwieldy and take longer to bring into action.

Overall, shotguns are unlikely to over penetrate and this is a consideration when you may be using the gun inside a house and do not want to endanger your family or neighbors. Most shotguns are unlikely to penetrate outside your dwelling but may go through an internal wall.

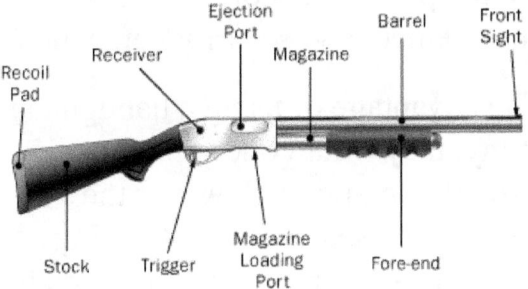

The component parts of the pup action shotgun

HANDGUNS

If a handgun is your preferred choice of defense weapon, then you need to consider the over penetration factor. Handguns, by their very nature are relatively short range firearms, and are the preferred choice for law enforcement and security personnel.

The advantage of using a handgun are many, they offer concealment and ease of operation. However they do need to be used competently. In effect, this means you need to practice with them and get to know them intimately. You may be able to hit a target when standing in front of a large bullseye or silhouette target that is not moving.

But could you be as accurate at night in a confined bedroom when an attacker is rushing at you?

If you are fortunate enough to live in a State that upholds the second Amendment, then you will need to consider the amount ammunition you carry and if a semi auto pistol, then the size of the magazine. You cannot anticipate that you will be facing only one attacker, and as we have seen, you cannot assume that one or two rounds on target will stop the individual who is threatening you. Therefore your handgun should be loaded with the maximum number of rounds it can hold. A spare magazine or speed-loader (In the case of a revolver) should be on hand in case needed.

Semi Auto Rifles

There is a growing popularity for the AR15 type semi auto rifle for home defense. These guns often called assault weapons by the press, have large capacity magazines, and are carried by most law enforcement officers as a backup. They have a number of features that make them a good choice. Like the Shotgun, they have a high fear factor and this means most attackers will be unlikely to remain in any location where one is being employed against them. Remember, the best result of any armed encounter is for the attacker/perpetrator to flee as fast as they can.

If the attacker is armed or wishes to engage you, then he is at a distinct disadvantage.

Most semi auto rifles such as the AK47 and AR15 are civilian versions of military firearms and can lay down a high rate of fire. Accurate to around 200 yards, the AR15 can empty a 20 round magazine in about the time you can fire 6 shots from your revolver.

So your choice of firearm is a personal matter for you as an individual. However, one aspect of defensive fire that we have not talked about, is Stopping power.

Stopping power is not an indication of the size of a gun, or its caliber. It is the ability of the shot to stop an attack by disabling or killing the attacker. Stopping power is as much about the type of bullet used as it is about the size of gun.

Most military ammunition is Full
Metal Jacket or FMJ

<u>Examples of full metal jacket as
opposed to hollow point bullets</u>

That means that the lead bullet is
encased inside a copper jacket.

These are designed to pass through the body leaving a small entrance hole and a slightly larger exit wound. The semi jacket hollow point is designed to expand and mushroom out when it strikes its target. This results in a large exit wound caused by the bullets erratic path, and there is higher damage to the internal organs.

Hunters know this and use soft point bullets to bring down a deer quickly. To illustrate this let me relate an incident that happened to me on our farm in Kentucky a few years back.

My wife and I had set up a metal oil drum as a burn barrel in the back yard. Once the oil drum was set up I decided to try out my new p38 on the barrel to put the required holes in it and test my new gun. At 5 yards I fired five 9mm rounds at it.

This resulted in 5 large dents in the metal. The ammunition I was using was soft lead nosed. I then reloaded the same gun with Full Metal Jacket and the results were stunning, five large entrance, and exit holes. The ammunition was 9mm and the powder charge equal in all rounds and I used the same pistol. The only difference was the bullets.

The full metal jacket had more speed but the lead bullet has greater impact stopping power. Most ammunition manufacturers produce personal defense rounds that are semi jacketed hollow-point. They will have high stopping power.

So having selected our weapon for home defense and got the training we need, what next?

CHAPTER NINE

INSIGHT

"Want of foresight, unwillingness to act when action would be simple and effective, lack of clear thinking, confusion of counsel until the emergency comes, until self-preservation strikes its jarring gong - these are the features which constitute the endless repetition of history."

Sir Winston Churchill

At the beginning of this book we related the tale of a single mom, Debbie who made a few basic mistakes in her home defense plan.

Now that you have had time to evaluate this, let us return to the story and see what Debbie could have done better.

Debbie left her gun locked in the gun safe; she also left her cell phone on charge in the living room. Had she plugged the charger into a socket in the bedroom when she got home from work, it would be now fully charged. When awoken she tried her phone and when it didn't work she switched on her bedside lamp, immediately alerting the intruder where she was. The intruder immediately burst into her room leaving her no time to access her handgun.

Your personal defense firearm must be accessible and loaded. Home invaders do not make appointments.

When awoken by the intruder, Debbie should have immediately called 911 and given her name and address plus the information that a **home invasion is in progress**. Do this as quietly as possible. She should have retrieved her handgun at the first available opportunity. Remember, the police will have your location and will be on route. If the intruder approaches your bedroom and attempts to come in, you should shout to him that you are armed and will fire if he enters. You need to shout clearly and forcefully, keeping the gun trained on the door. If he enters then you must shoot; aim for the center mass i.e. the torso. The law allows you to shoot, if you feel under threat. It does not make a difference if the intruder is armed or just threatening.

You would be justified in shooting as many times as required to stop the threat. Should the intruder heed your warning and run away, you are not legally allowed to pursue and shoot him. In the event of the intruder fleeing the house before you have a chance to call 911, then you must immediately call and give them the details. If you fired at him but missed, that should also be relayed to the dispatcher. Remember, the 911 tape will be examined and checked against your account of the incident.

It is a very good idea to have a sheet of paper next to your phone with your Name, Address and phone number, and possibly number of family members and pets in the house. When you are stressed, it is amazing what you will forget.

You should make an effort to clean and service your firearm regularly, even when it is in storage. Avoid leaving a loaded magazine in the gun for long periods. This may compress the spring to a point that it will not feed the rounds smoothly and that will cause a jam or malfunction. It can also warp or expand the magazine itself and cause the magazine to stick during ejection or insertion into the magazine well.

If you find that the magazine does not insert or eject smoothly, have it repaired or replaced.

Make sure that all ammunition is clean and there is no corrosion on the cases. This will insure that the ammo inserts into the chamber smoothly and ejects smoothly. Even handling ammo can cause the start of corrosion.

If you would like to contact either of us concerning questions you may have concerning what you have read in this book, please feel free to drop us an email to;
harmonyhollow@hotmail.com

www.ingramcontent.com/pod-product-compliance
Lightning Source LLC
Chambersburg PA
CBHW051700170526
45167CB00002B/470